ABSOLUTE BEGINNERS

Bass Guitar

OMNIBUS EDITION

AMSCO PUBLICATIONS

New York/London/Paris/Sydney/Copenhagen/Berlin/Madrid/Hong Kong/Tokyo

Exclusive Distributor for the United States, Canada, Mexico and U.S. possessions:
Hal Leonard Corporation
7777 West Bluemound Road, Milwaukee, WI 53213 USA

Exclusive Distributors for the rest of the World:
Music Sales Limited
14-15 Berners Street, London W1T 3LJ England
Music Sales Pty. Limited
20 Resolution Drive, Caringbah, NSW 2229, Australia

Order No. AM 1001627
ISBN 978.0.8256.3756.8
HL Item Number:14037744

Written by Phil Mulford
Cover and text photographs by George Taylor
Other photographs courtesy of LFI/Redferns/WireImage
Book design by Chloë Alexander
Models: Jim Benham (Book 1) and Simone Butler (Book 2)

Printed in the United States of America by
Vicks Lithograph and Printing Corporation

Book 1 Contents

Introduction

This book will guide you through from the
very first time you take your bass out of its case,
right through to playing bass parts to complete songs.

Easy-to-follow instructions
will guide you through
• how to look after your bass
• how to tune it
• learning your first notes
• playing your first song

Play along with the backing track as you learn –
the specially recorded audio will let you hear
how the music should sound—then try playing
the part yourself.

Practice regularly and often.
Twenty minutes every day
is far better than two hours
on the weekend with
nothing in-between.

Not only are you training your
brain to understand how to play
the bass, you are also teaching
your muscles to memorize
certain repeated actions.

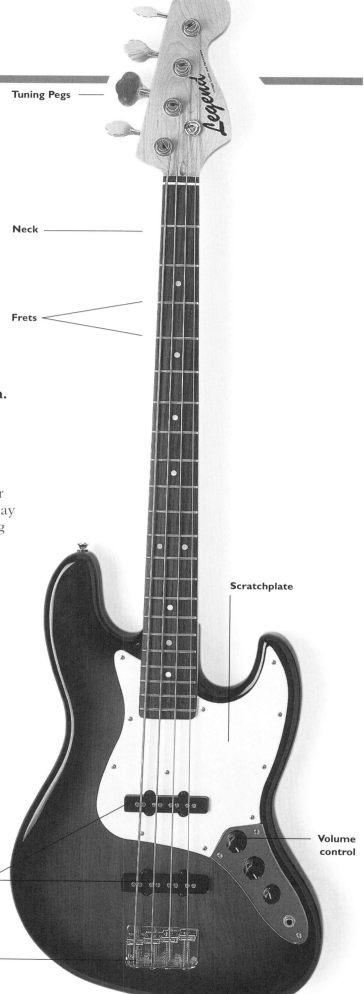

Tuning Pegs

Neck

Frets

Scratchplate

Volume
control

Pick-ups

Bridge

Tone controls

Track 1 on **CD1 (Track 1-1)** gives you the correct notes for you to tune each string of your bass. You'll hear each of the bass's open strings in turn, starting with the bottom string.

You can alter the tightness (and therefore the pitch) of each string by twisting the tuning pegs at the top of the neck.

A bass can also be tuned with pitch-pipes, a tuning fork, an electronic tuner, or by tuning to another instrument such as a piano. Once one string is in tune the others can be tuned to it.

Let's assume the bottom E is correctly tuned. Hold down the 5th fret on that string to get an A.

Now play the open A string—they should sound the same. If the A string is higher or lower, tune it down a little or up until they are the same. As they get closer in pitch you may hear a strange oscillating or "beating" tone generated by the two notes. The oscillation rate decreases as the notes become closer in pitch.

Repeat the process at the 5th fret for the D string and G string.

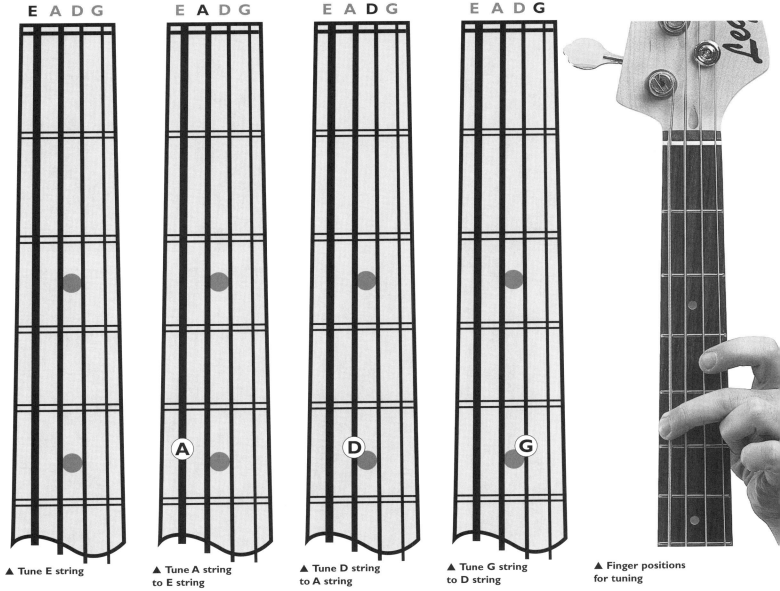

▲ Tune E string

▲ Tune A string to E string

▲ Tune D string to A string

▲ Tune G string to D string

▲ Finger positions for tuning

Position and posture

In order to play well you must be comfortable with your instrument.

Holding the Bass
Start with your bass at about waist level, relaxing your shoulders by rolling them back a little.

Check your playing position in a mirror and compare it to the photos on these pages.

It's important to keep the neck of the bass pointing upward a little.

Mani
Stone Roses &
Primal Scream

Nicky Wire
Manic Street
Preachers

Sting

Every bassist has a slightly different posture—just check out the photos of bassists used throughout this book to see the variety of possible playing positions. Experiment with the length of the strap until your left and right hands feel comfortable—a higher position may make playing slightly easier, but a low-slung bass often looks much cooler!

If you plan to play standing up for any length of time a good quality strap will help you avoid discomfort. A soft, wide strap is best, as the width helps to spread the weight of the instrument.

Plucking

You have two choices on how to produce notes on the bass: either

- pluck with the first two fingers (usually alternating)

or

- use a pick

Pick or Fingers?

Your choice will probably depend on the type of music you want to play—if you want to play in a jazz or soul group, you should probably use your fingers.

If, on the other hand, you want to play in a metal or rock band you'll need to use a pick to make yourself heard!

With Fingers

Using your first two fingers in an alternating style takes some practice. Start slowly. Then you can speed up and your playing will remain accurate.

Your thumb can be anchored on the bass, on the side of the pickup, the scratchplate or on the chrome pickup cover if your bass has one. The photos below show how your fingers should look.

▲ ▶ **Possible right hand plucking positions**

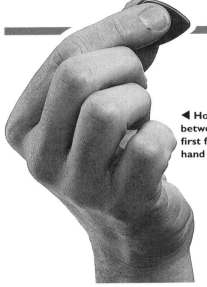

◀ Hold the pick firmly between your thumb and first finger, keeping your right hand and arm relaxed.

With a Pick

Picks come in different thicknesses—thin, medium or heavy. Each gives a different sound and feels different when playing. For bass, heavy picks tend to be best as they are less likely to flex as you hit the strings.

Practice striking the open strings of your bass with the pick—you can strike the string once on the way towards the floor (a "downstroke") and again on the way back up (an "upstroke").
Try to hit the string with the same force on the way down and on the way up—this will ensure that you get an even feel.

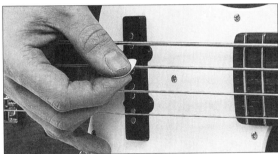

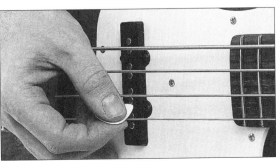

◀ Starting a downstroke on each string

▲ Playing with the pick

Left hand position

Place your left hand over the fretboard, with your thumb on the back of the neck roughly behind your middle finger.

You should always aim to use one finger per fret—practice stretching your fingers, as shown in the photo. If you find this a difficult stretch on the lower frets, try the same position above the 5th fret, where the frets are closer together.

The photo below demonstrates a poor hand position—notice how the fingers are all bunched together.

Using one finger per fret may seem tiring at first—but persevere and you will soon build up strength in your hand. If you feel your hand getting tired, take it off the fretboard, let your arm hang down by your side and relax completely. You should never continue practicing if your hand is hurting as it can cause permanent damage.

▶ **Paul McCartney—possibly the most famous left-handed bassist of all time.**

Tip

The left-handed guitarist
Left handed players should simply reverse all the instructions in this book—your fretting hand will be the right hand, and your plucking hand will be the left.

Red Hot Chili Peppers' bassist Flea is known for performing backward somersaults while playing his bass!

First steps

Here's your first piece, laid out on the standard music staff and with a system called tablature.

The Staff
Traditionally, music is written on five lines, called a "staff." On these lines and spaces notes are written, indicating pitch and rhythm.

If a note is too high or too low for the staff an extra short line is added, called a "leger" line.

The important leger line note for bass is the one that represents the lowest E.

Check out the diagram below to see how different notes are represented on the staff.

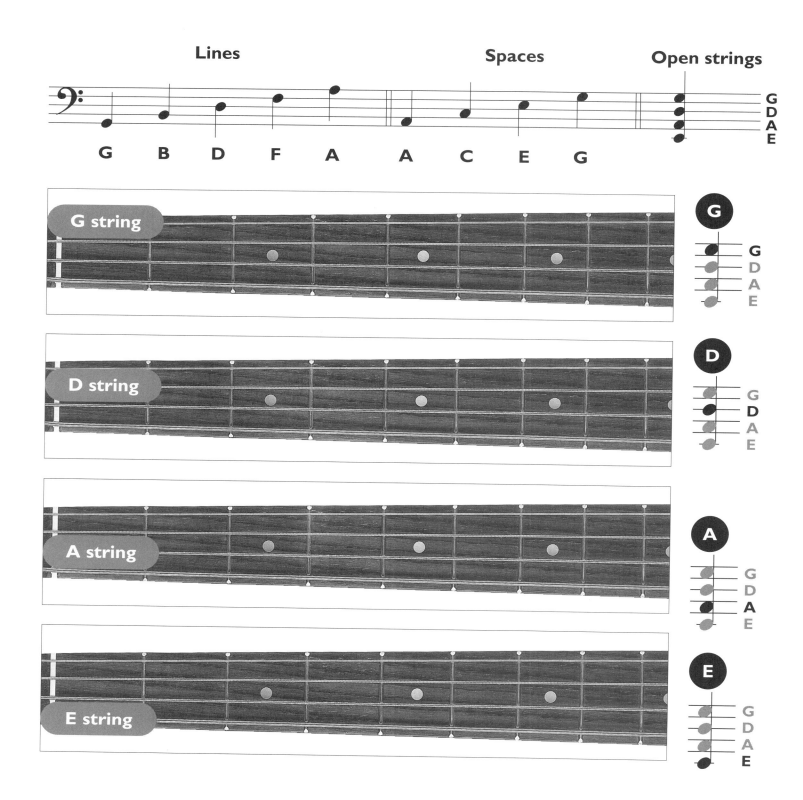

The good news for bassists is that you don't need to worry about the musical staff, because "tablature" will tell you exactly where to find each note on the fretboard. Tablature (or TAB) is always given under the traditional musical notation.

The four horizontal lines represent the four strings of your bass. The lowest line represents the bottom string, and the highest the top string.

The numbers on the horizontal lines tell you exactly which string and which fret you need to produce the note that you want! The only thing that TAB can't give you is the rhythm—you'll still need to refer to the staff for that.

Try finding some of the notes indicated by the TAB in this example:

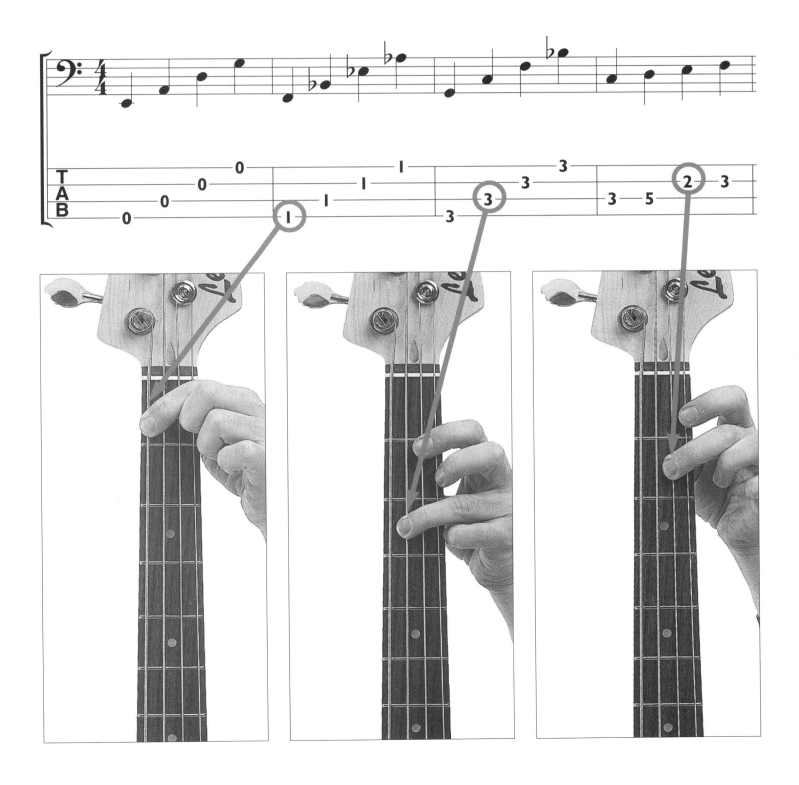

Your first note A

Let's start right away with your first bass line—this track can be played all the way through using one open string!

Listen to **Track 1-2** to hear how the bass fits in with the rest of the band—it simply plays the open A string (the 3rd string) on the first beat of each bar. The drummer's bass (or kick) drum is also struck on this beat, so listen to that and try and hit your note at exactly the same time.

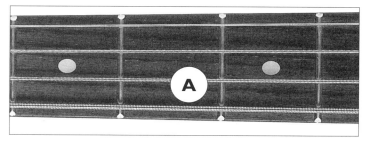

▲ **Open A string**

Rhythmically, the note you are playing is known as a quarter note. Count 1-2-3-4 as you play and then pluck or pick the open A string as you count "1." Play the note for one beat only, then stop it by resting your finger on it as you count "2."

Once you're familiar with the tune, try playing along with **Track 1-3**—remember to play rhythmically and with confidence—it's your role to provide the foundation of the track, so you've got to be rock steady!

Song structure

This tune has 3 sections:
Sections A and C are identical, so we'll call them the *Verse* sections.
Section B has a different harmony, so we'll call that the *Middle* section.

The rhythm section

The bass player and the drummer together form what is known as the "rhythm section"—they lock together to provide a steady pulse over which the rest of the band can play. Get into the habit of listening carefully to how drummers and bassists work together to produce a groove.

▼ **Led Zeppelin's rhythm section—John Paul Jones on bass and John Bonham on drums.**

From A to E

This second tune moves from the open A string to the open bottom string E.

Instead of only playing on the first beat, you're now going to play on each of the four beats in the bar. Once again, the bass drum is struck on each of these beats—so listen for it and try and lock in exactly with that rhythm. As you're not using your fretting hand to hold down notes, this is an ideal opportunity to concentrate on what your plucking hand is doing. Experiment with alternate down/up strokes with the pick, or pluck with your first and second fingers.

Whichever method you use, try to make sure that you keep the notes separate and consistent in volume.

Track 1-4 demonstrates how the bass part should sound.

Track 1-5 is your chance to play along.

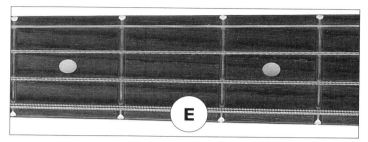

▲ **Open E string**

Speed up your learning

Some hints to help you practice:

1 Try to find time to practice every day—even if it's only for 10 minutes. It's much better to practice every day for 10 minutes than it is to practice once a week for two hours!

2 Listen and learn! Try to pick out the bass parts to your favorite tracks, and hear how the bass player fits in with the rest of the band.

3 Start slowly! Once you've perfected the part, you can then speed up— and your rhythm will remain steady.

You've used the bottom E and A strings—now it's time for the D string and a new rhythm.
This tune is a classic groove which you'll always find useful. It uses an eighth note as the second note in each bar. The eighth note is half as long as a quarter note.

Listen to **Track 1-6** to hear how it sounds.

Count a steady four in a bar and try to play this rhythm - you should find that the eighth note falls in between beats 2 and 3.

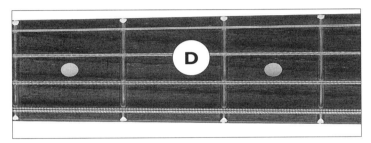

▲ **Open D string**

If you insert an "and" in between each beat as you count, you'll find it even easier to fit the eighth note in:

1 & 2 **& 3** & 4 &

You should play on the beats underlined. Once you've mastered this rhythm, try playing along with **Track 1-7**.

This tune has an Intro (section A), with sections B, C and E as Verses, and D as a Middle for contrast.

Listen to the way that your bass notes sound different as the chords change over it.

Off-beats and syncopation
The "ands" that you've just been counting fall in between the main beats of the bar, and are known as *off-beats*. Playing on off-beats makes a bass part much more interesting—in fact there's a special musical term for it—*syncopation*.

Right hand plucking position

Middle

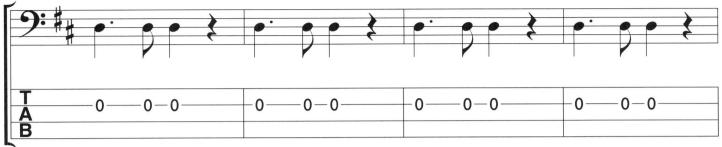

Verse 3

Your first 12-bar blues

Next up, let's play some blues.

This 12-bar chord sequence has been used for thousands of songs in blues, pop, rock and many other types of music—once you're familiar with it you'll start to recognize it everywhere.

Here we're going to take the bass rhythm from the previous tune and play the open string which relates to each chord.

The first four bars are on A, so that's what we play. In bar 5 the chord changes to D, so we change to D too—and so on. The whole 12-bar sequence can be played with just the open E, A and D strings.

Listen to **Track 1-8**

and then play along with **Track 1-9**.

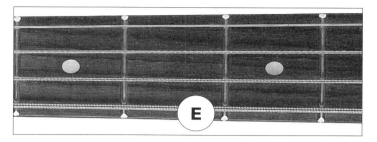

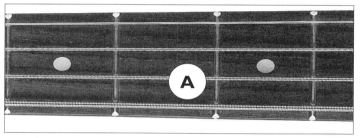

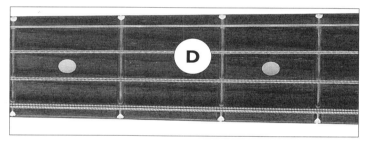

Tip

If you get tired, take a break, let your plucking hand relax and then try again. As you practice you'll build up more strength in your hands, and you'll be able to play for longer.

▼ **Cream (bassist Jack Bruce, drummer Ginger Baker and guitarist Eric Clapton) prepare to tackle another 12-bar blues.**

2 bars click in

The symbol :|| at the end of bar 12 is known as the repeat sign—once you reach that sign you should return to the beginning of the example and start again. The second time through ignore the sign and go on to the last bar.

CHECKPOINT

WHAT YOU'VE ACHIEVED SO FAR...

You can now:
• Position your right and left hands properly
• Pluck or pick the strings
• Tune your bass
• Read simple TAB
• Play the open E, A and D strings
• Play bass lines in time with a backing track
• Understand simple off-beat rhythms

Playing with both hands

So far you've only used open strings—now it's time to put your fretting hand into action.

Finding your way

All musicians practice sequences of notes known as scales to give them greater finger strength, speed and flexibility—and bassists are no exception.

The diagram on the right shows the fretboard pattern for a C major scale.

C major

• All major scales consist of 7 notes—C major uses the notes C D E F G A and B.
• C major is named after the note that it starts on—C!
• The major scale forms a particular pattern on the fretboard—you'll soon come across other patterns such as the *minor* and the *pentatonic*.

Listen to **Track 1-10** and follow the TAB given below— this is known as the scale of C major.

Play each note four times in a bar, along with the drum groove (**Track 1-11**).
Use alternate first finger/second finger plucking or alternate strokes of the pick.

▼ **Starting position for C major scale**

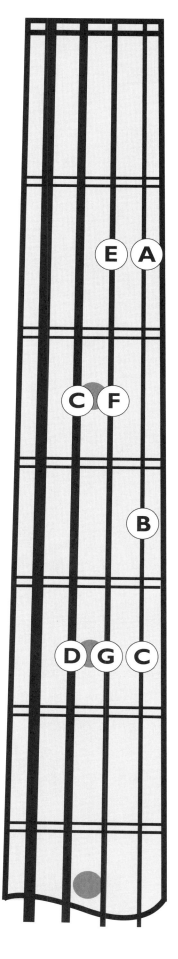

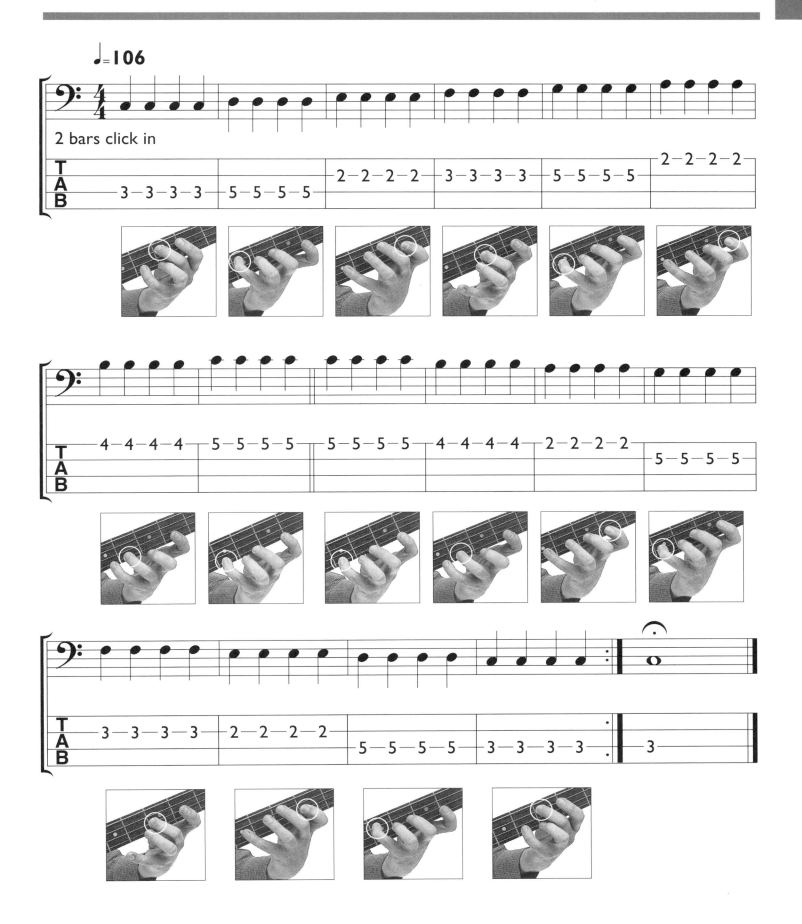

Speed it up!

Now we're going to take the same finger pattern but play each note only once.

Listen to **Track 1-12** to hear how this should sound.

You'll have to think quickly to be able to play this in time—start slowly and gradually build up speed, until you're ready to play along with **Track 1-13**.

So far, all the bass lines you've played have used root notes—they're the bottom notes of the chords under which you're playing.

But you can also use the other notes of those chords to spice up your bass lines...

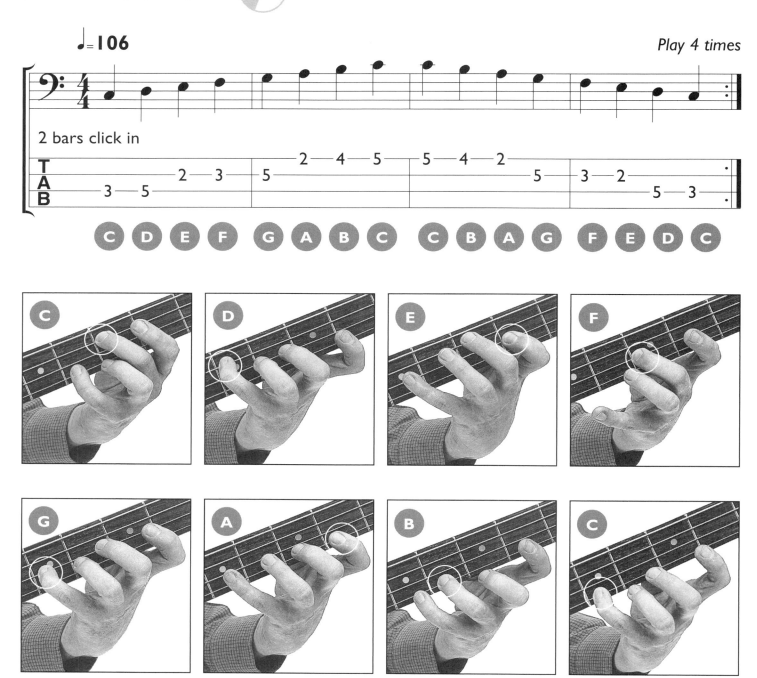

An arpeggio of C major is created when we play the 1st, 3rd, 5th and then the 8th note of the C major scale: C E G and then C again.

The example below (**Track 1-14**) shows you how to play this arpeggio, based on the C major scale pattern you learned previously.

Refer to the fingerings shown in the photos—start slowly and build up speed until you can play along with **Track 1-15**.

Movable patterns

Because you're not playing any open strings this pattern can be moved to any position on the neck—it's known as a movable pattern.

This means that if you wanted a D major arpeggio you could just move the whole pattern up two frets. In fact, using this pattern you can play any major chord shape you want!

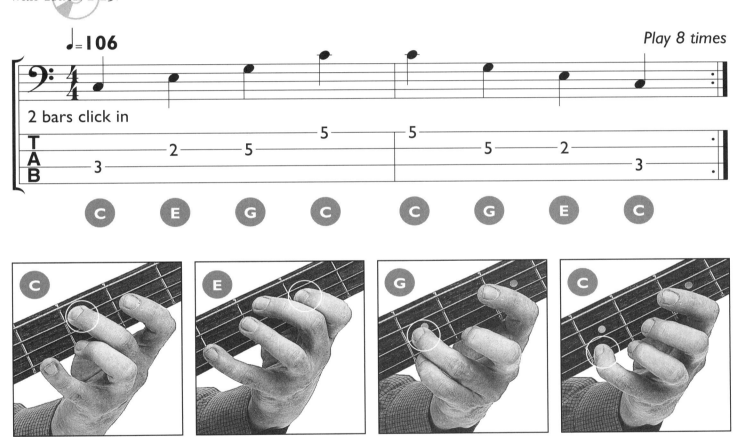

Chords & Arpeggios

When a guitarist plays a chord—he (or she) is generally playing at least 3 different notes simultaneously. Try this on your bass—it doesn't sound great, does it? The lower pitch of the bass guitar means that chords just don't sound very good. But if you split chords up and play each note separately you create an arpeggio—and they are ideal for creating bass lines.

Tip

The top two notes can be played either with your third and fourth finger, or by using the little finger to hold both notes down on the first and second strings.

Minor arpeggios

You can do the exactly the same thing with minor chords. The example below gives you an arpeggio of A minor, starting on the bottom E string.

Listen to **Track 1-16**—try to hear the difference between this minor pattern, and the major pattern you've just played.

Minor chords have a much darker, gloomy sound—in contrast to the bright feel of a major chord.

Once again, start very slowly and work out exactly where your fingers should fall—then gradually speed up until you can play along with **Track 1-17**.

Tip

This is also a movable pattern. Simply move the shape up or down the fretboard to get any minor arpeggio you want.

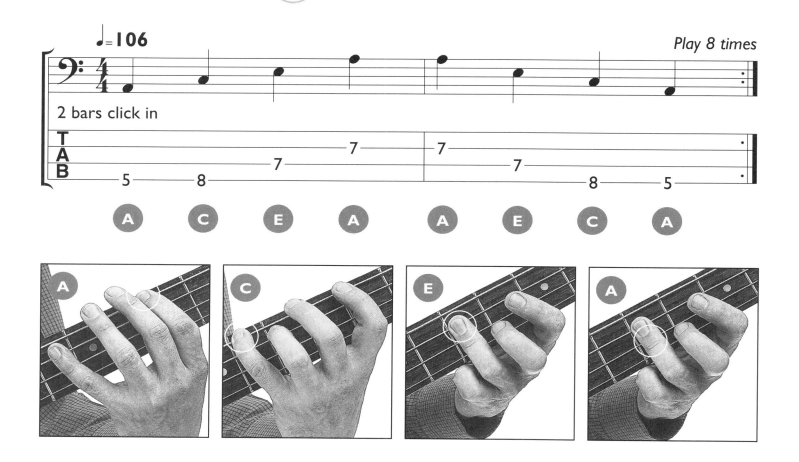

▲ **Left hand position**

Let's give your fretting hand a rest, and concentrate on your plucking hand.

This example will really test your stamina!

There's only one note to worry about here—a low G —the challenge will be to keep the rhythm steady and even.

Listen to **Track 1-18** to hear what it should sound like!

When you're happy with your right hand technique, try playing along with **Track 1-19**.

You're playing eighth notes so there are 8 in each bar —two on each beat. Count 1 & 2 & 3 & 4 & steadily through each bar and pluck/pick steadily—aim to produce an even volume on each note.

▲ **Right hand plucking position**

▲ **Right hand picking position**

Tip

Try practicing with a metronome.
Start around 70 b.p.m. (beats per minute) and then gradually
increase the speed until you get up to 100.
You'll need to play two notes
for every click of the metronome.

Make sure that your left hand and arm don't become tense—relax and let your arm hang naturally.

Here's another example to test your stamina, this time using the note B♭ on the first fret of the 3rd string.

Track 1-20 gives you a demonstration.

Track 1-21 is the backing track.

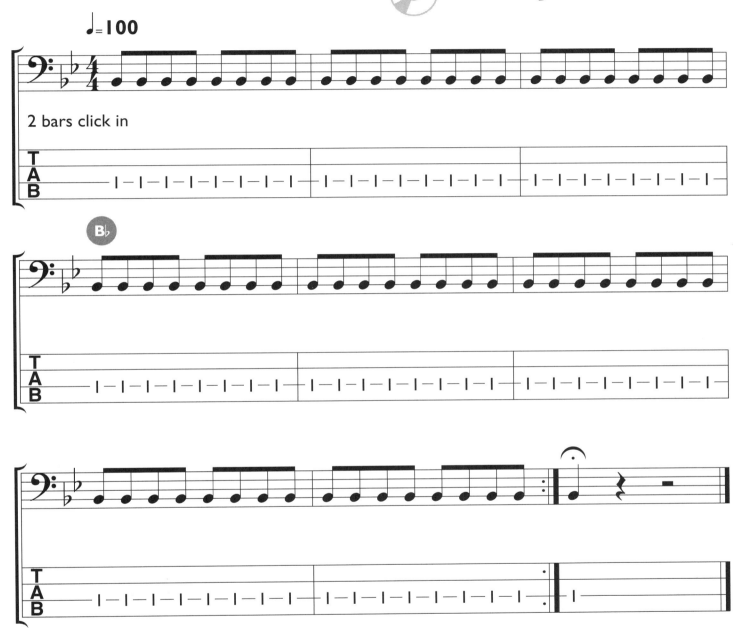

2 bars click in

Left hand position for **B♭**

CHECKPOINT

WHAT YOU'VE ACHIEVED SO FAR...

You can now:

• Play a major scale pattern

• Play major and minor arpeggios

• Maintain steady plucking rhythms at fast speeds

Playing songs

To finish, we're going to apply all the basic ideas you've learned to a couple of tunes.

The first example is a midtempo "down-home" blues. It has a shuffle feel, as if each beat is dividing into three rather than two—listen to **Track 1-22**—you'll recognize this rhythm right away.

The example is a 12-bar in the key of E – you tackled a blues in A back on page 23 so you should be familiar with the structure.

Note that the chords for each bar are written above the staff—this helps you to know which notes you could play other than just the root note.

Use the arpeggio exercise to work out where you can play A, D and E as arpeggio figures and then experiment putting them in the right bars.

1st & 2nd ending bars

The symbol at the end of bar 12 is known as the repeat sign—once you reach that sign you should return to the beginning of the example and start again. Now, check out the brackets above bars 11 and 12—these tell you that you should use those bars on the first and second times through the blues only—this will lead you to the repeat sign once more—so return to the top for the third and final time. On the third time you need to leave out the 1st and 2nd ending bars and skip straight to the 3rd ending bar, which will take you to the end of the piece—otherwise you'll end up going round and round in circles!

Once you're confident with the changes, try playing along with **Track 1-23**.

▼ **P-Funk's Bootsy Collins—one of the funkiest bassists of all time.**

Tip

Watch out for the last bar of the 12— it's a little bit more complicated. Isolate that bar and practice it slowly— it's a classic blues phrase that's used to round off the piece.

see photographs below for finger positions

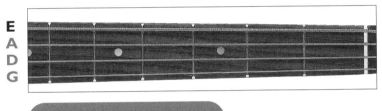

E open string

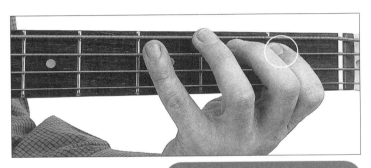

A♯ finger position

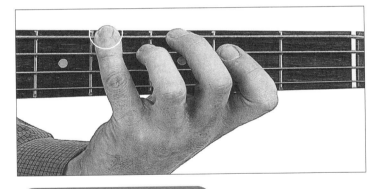

G♯ finger position

B finger position

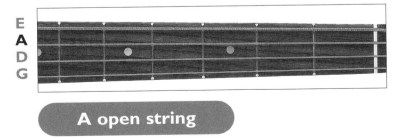

A open string

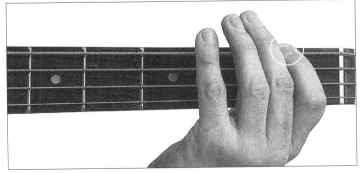

F finger position

This last tune is a much longer rock number in the key of G.

It has a four-bar intro before you come in on bass—listen to **Track 1-24** and try to familiarize yourself with the structure of the song (like the previous example, it uses first and second ending bars).

The first 4 bars of the track don't have a bass part—so count carefully and be ready to come in at letter A.

The Verse section uses the following 5 notes—if you follow the fingerings indicated in these photos you should find that they fall under your fingers easily.

When you reach section B you'll find the bass part breaks into "pumping" eighth notes.

Section B uses exactly the same finger positions as the verse.

Section C is a repeat of the intro but this time you do join in. You then play sections A and B again, (with the second time ending), which will then take you to section E, the outro.

Here are the fret and finger positions for section E.

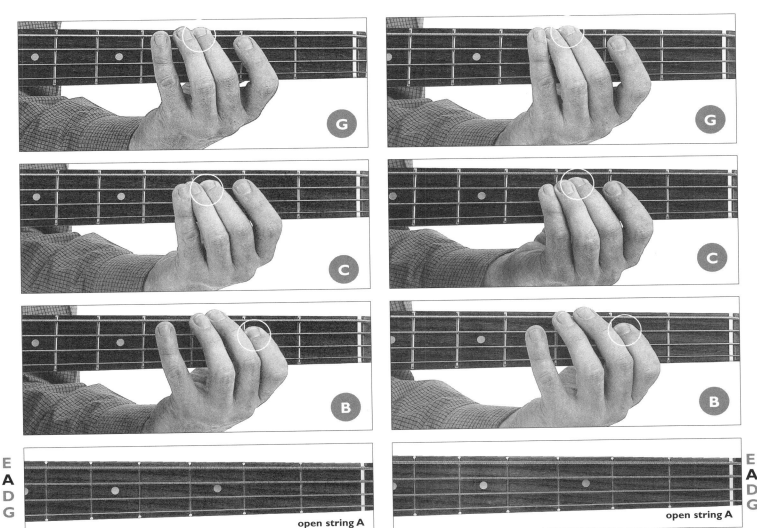

Track 1-25 is your chance to shine, as you play a complete bass line along with the backing track.

Let it rock!

Tip

Watch out for bars 8 and 12 where the
chord changes halfway through the bar—try
to think ahead, and be prepared for each
chord change before it happens.

Congratulations!

You've made a good start in bass playing. The skills and techniques you've learned in this book will form the foundation of your bass playing in the future.

If you want to take your bass playing further, then continue on to Book Two, and spend some time listening to the bass playing of the musicians featured in this book.

FINAL CHECKPOINT

You've now covered all the basics of bass playing. You can:

• Tune your bass
• Read tablature
• Play scales and arpeggios
• Play 12-bar sequences in A and E
• Play fast repeated 8th note and syncopated rhythms
• Play complete bass lines to two songs

The Who's **John Entwistle** and **Roger Daltrey**

Alex James
Blur

Adam Clayton
U2

Mani
Stone Roses

Here are some classic but simple bass lines that you should now be able to approach. Most are simple enough to pick up straight off the recording!

Another One Bites The Dust Queen
Design For Life Manic Street Preachers
Parklife Blur
Shakermaker Oasis
She Bangs The Drums Stone Roses
Smoke On The Water Deep Purple
Walking On The Moon Sting
With Or Without You U2
You Really Got Me The Kinks

ABSOLUTE BEGINNERS
Bass Guitar
K TWO

Book 2 Contents

Introduction

Welcome to **Absolute Beginners Bass Book Two.**

This book is perfect for you if you've just finished *Absolute Beginners Bass Guitar* (Book One), or have a few bass guitar skills already. It explores new grooves and techniques essential to your growth as a musician and bass player.

In *Absolute Beginners Bass Guitar* (Book One) you will have studied:

- Tuning the bass

- Position and posture

- Plucking and picking

- Fretting hand position

- Open strings

- Tablature and notation

- Quarter and eighth note grooves

- C major scale

- C major and A minor arpeggios

- Plucking hand stamina

- 12 bar blues sequence in the keys of A and E

- Playing straight eight and shuffle rhythms

- Playing a complete song with two different grooves

You will need to have studied all of the points above to get the most from this book.

About the CD
The tracks are arranged with a full demonstration first, then without bass for you to play along with. Sometimes there is a slower play-along example. Tempos are notated relative to a quarter note. E.g.: "♩ = 120" means 120 quarter notes per minute. That's two beats per second.

Tuning
The open strings are tuned to E, A, D and G.
Track 1 on **CD2 (Track 2-1)** on the CD is a reference A, the open second string.

Why do we use the open A string?
An orchestra tunes up to concert A, played by an oboe.

Concert A = 440 HZ (HZ= Hertz = vibrations per second). So in respect of that, we start with an A.

Next we need to tune the other strings in relation to the A.

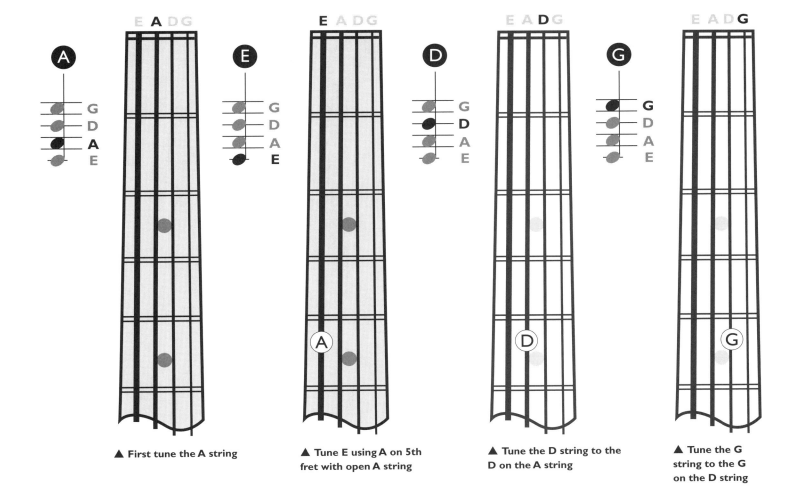

▲ First tune the A string

▲ Tune E using A on 5th fret with open A string

▲ Tune the D string to the D on the A string

▲ Tune the G string to the G on the D string

Do practice tuning your bass without an electronic tuner. This will help you develop your sense of pitch and help you to hear the notes when copying bass lines.

Tip
Try to sing the note pitches as you tune up.
This will help you develop a good ear.

Position and posture

Make sure you are as comfortable as possible when you play. If you plan a long practice session, then sit down and take the weight off your body. Wear a strap at all times to keep the bass in a comfortable position.

If you do wear the bass very low, standing is the only option.

Make sure you have a wide, soft strap to spread the weight and keep a straight back with your shoulders relaxed.

The plucking hand
At this stage we need to be getting our fingers and picks in order! You don't want to be tripping up on your killer riff.

With fingers
It's best to anchor on the side of the pickup. This means you can "dig in" to your grooves by pulling against the pickup cover. You may also move your thumb over to mute the E string when playing higher up on the bass.

With a pick

You will, by now, have a favorite shape and gauge of pick. Make sure you hold it between your thumb and index finger.

When practicing, work on your up and down strokes. They should be even in timing and tone; we don't want sloppy pick work upsetting the groove!

Here is an exercise to make sure your finger or pick work is always in the pocket.
Use alternating fingers, or up and down strokes.

Listen to the slowed down demonstration track on **Track 2-2**, then play along with the band in **Track 2-3**, also at the slower tempo (♩ = 92).

When you have mastered this, move up to speed with **Track 2-4** (♩ = 112).

This next exercise will help get those shuffle eights in order.
Track 2-5 is the full demonstration track and **Track 2-6** is the backing only.
Both are at the slower tempo of ♩ = 96.

When you feel ready, move on to **Track 2-7**, which is at the faster speed of ♩ = 114.

Shuffle

Practice time

Be organized.
You need to use your time efficiently. Work out a
practice schedule like the one below:

Subject	Percentage of time
1. Warming up	15%
2. Scales and arpeggios	15%
3. Listen!	35%
4. Play	35%

1. Warming up
Just as athletes exercise gently before a competition,
we need to loosen those fingers up before a gig or
rehearsal, especially if your hands are cold.

The previous tracks are a good starting place for your
plucking hand. For your fingerboard skills however,
we need to try some awkward finger combinations.

Track 2-8 is the demonstration track at the faster
tempo (♩ = 96),

Track 2-9 is the slowed down backing track (♩ = 82),

then **Track 2-10** is the backing track at full speed.

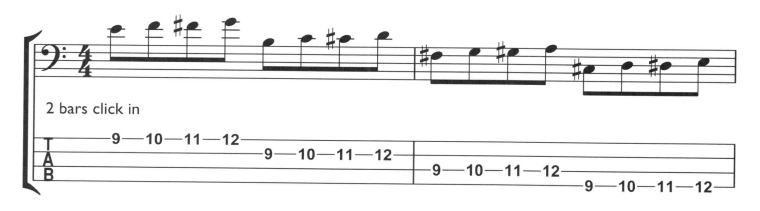

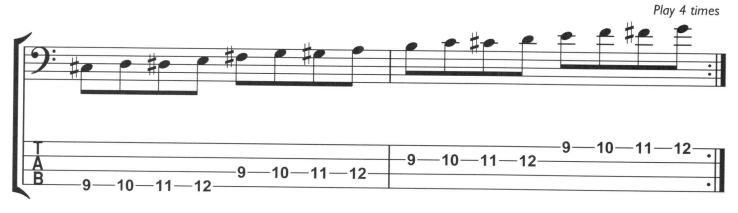

2. Scales and arpeggios

It is good practice to run up and down some scales and arpeggios in different positions. Use a steady rhythm to play with.

3. Listen!

Check out a track you want to copy and have your bass handy to work out the pitch of the notes. It is good to sing the bass lines to help you hear the intervals. Some good quality headphones will help you to listen to the bass.

4. Play

Practice the song you are studying. Split it up into sections: Intro, Verse, Chorus, Bridge, Middle, etc., then practice and memorize each section and the order in which they come in the song. Next, try the whole thing, remember your mistakes, correct them, and then move on to another song. You can never learn too many!

Tip

Practice little but often. Practicing for 12 hours will not turn you into a great musician more quickly – you'll just get sore hands.

Flea from Red Hot Chili Peppers

Major scales

Unlock the fingerboard

The strings on the bass are tuned in 4ths, so any riff or pattern can be moved to change its key.

C major in three positions

In *Absolute Beginners Bass Guitar* (Book One) p.25, we played the C major scale starting on fret 3 of the A string. We can also play the same-pitched notes starting at fret 8 of the E string.

C scale (8th fret, E string)

By learning scales and arpeggios in different positions we can increase our knowledge of the fingerboard to give greater flexibility.

Track 2-11 is the demonstration track at the faster tempo (♩ = 96), **Track 2-12** is the slowed down backing track (♩ = 82), then **Track 2-13** is the backing track at full speed.

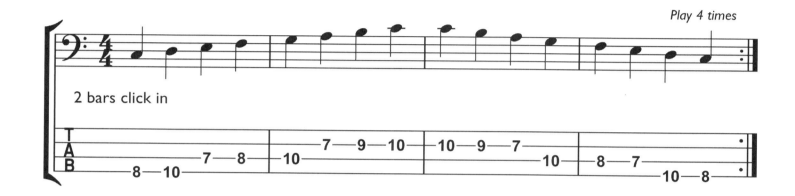

Play 4 times

2 bars click in

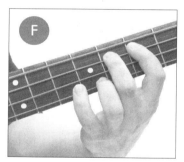

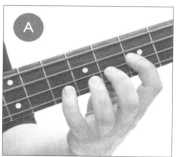
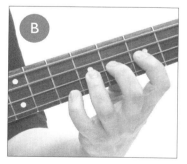

To take C major up an octave (to the next higher pitch, but in the same key) start on fret 15 of the A string and repeat the major scale pattern. You have just increased your fingerboard knowledge two-fold!

C scale (15th fret, A string)
Track **2-14** is the demonstration track at the faster tempo (♩ = 96), **Track 2-15** is the slowed down backing track (♩ = 82), then **Track 2-16** is the backing track at full speed.

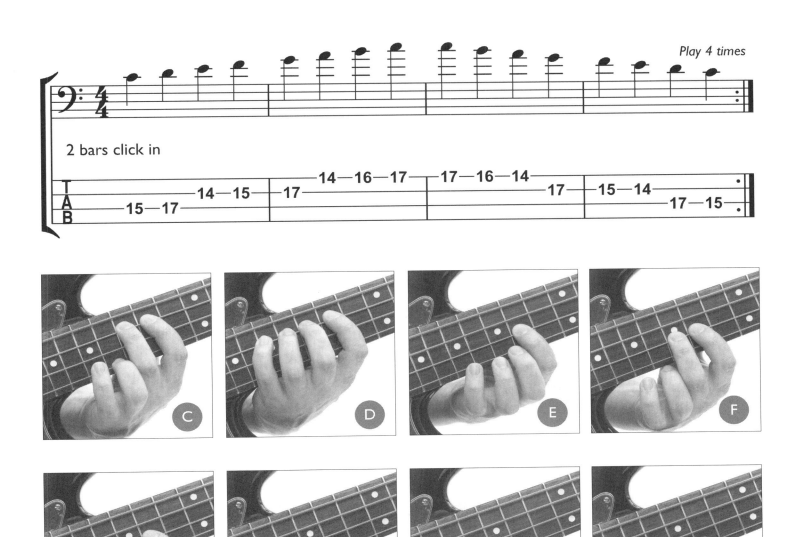

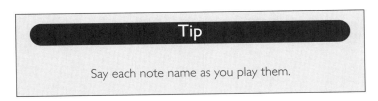

Tip

Say each note name as you play them.

Minor scales

C dorian minor scale

There are several types of minor scales. The one most commonly used in Western popular music is the minor 7th scale which evolved from a group of scales called *modes*. No need to make things too complicated, but we have here a scale with a minor 3rd and a flatted 7th.

The modal name for this scale is *dorian*. This scale applies to all minor and minor 7th chords with a natural 5th.

Track 2-17 is the demonstration at the faster tempo (♩ = 96), **Track 2-18** is the slowed down backing track (♩ = 82), then **Track 2-19** is the backing track at full speed.

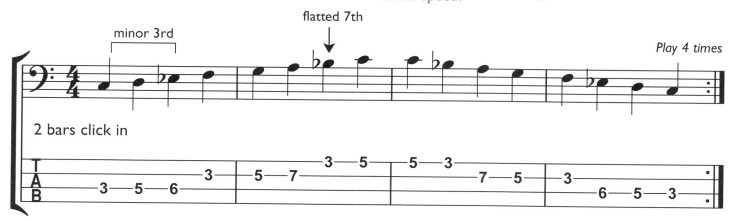

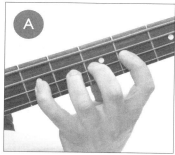
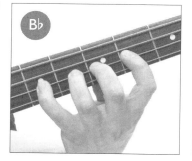

Tip

Practice this alongside the C major scale. Listen to how different they sound.

C major arpeggio, position two

Now we are going to move the C major arpeggio to other positions to expand our knowledge further. We are going to start on the 8th fret of the E string, where we started the C major scale on page 10.

Track 2-20 is the demonstration at the faster tempo (♩ = 96). Track 2-21 is the slowed down backing track (♩ = 82), then Track 2-22 is the backing track at full speed.

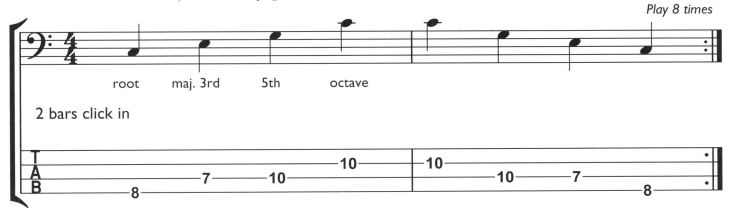

C major arpeggio, position three

Practice this C major arpeggio at fret 15 of the A string.

Track 2-23 is the demonstration at the faster tempo (♩ = 96).

Track 2-24 is the slowed down backing track (♩ = 82), then Track 2-25 is the backing track at full speed.

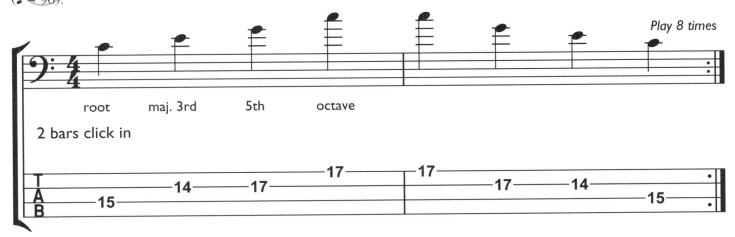

Minor arpeggios

A minor arpeggio, position two

Now let's move the position of the minor arpeggios. This time we are playing the A minor arpeggio that we covered in *Absolute Beginners Bass Guitar* (Book One), p.28. We will start with the open string A. This A is the same pitch as fret 5 of the E string.

Track 2-26 is the demonstration at the faster tempo (♩ = 96), **Track 2-27** is the slowed down backing track (♩ = 82), then **Track 2-28** is the backing track at full speed.

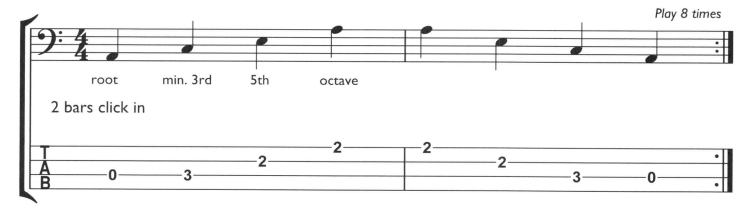

root   min. 3rd   5th   octave

2 bars click in

Play 8 times

A

C

E

A

A minor arpeggio, position three

We are now going to move the A minor arpeggio up in pitch to the next octave. This is the same pattern as A minor using the open strings, except that we start on the 12th fret.

Track 2-29 is the demonstration at the faster tempo (♩ = 96), **Track 2-30** is the slowed down backing track (♩ = 82), then **Track 2-31** is the backing track at full speed.

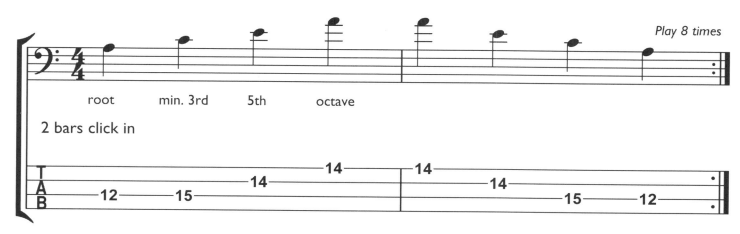

root   min. 3rd   5th   octave

2 bars click in

Play 8 times

A

C

E

A

In addition to the major scales, we need to know the dominant 7th scale and its structure. This scale has a flatted 7th note, which means the 7th note is one fret lower than the 7th in the major scale. The result is a more edgy and bluesy sounding scale. Here is the C dominant 7th scale:

Track 2-32 is the demonstration at the faster tempo (♩ = 96), **Track 2-33** is the slowed down backing track (♩ = 82), then **Track 2-34** is the backing track at full speed.

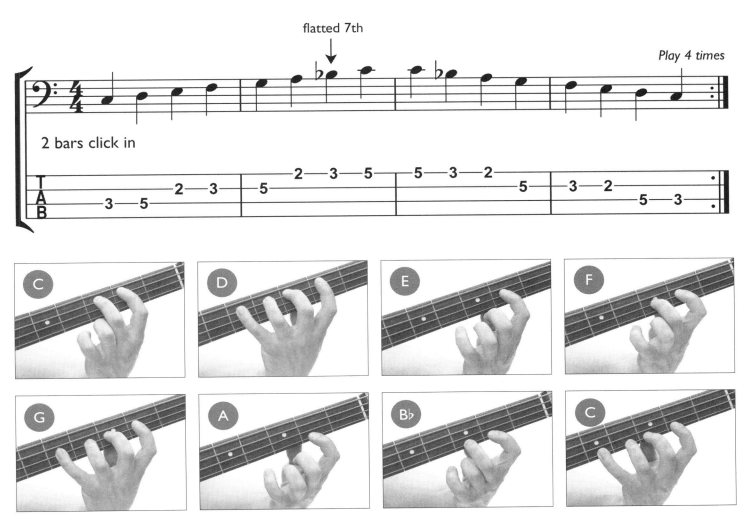

flatted 7th

Play 4 times

2 bars click in

CHECKPOINT

WHAT YOU'VE ACHIEVED SO FAR...

You can now:
1. Tune up from concert A
2. Warm up both hands
3. Practice in an organized fashion
4. Play major and minor scales in different fretboard positions
5. Play major and minor arpeggios in different fretboard positions
6. Play dominant 7th scales

The pentatonic scale

Scales and arpeggios are the backbone of your playing. Thorough knowledge of them is important and helps you to find your way around the fingerboard.

Pentatonic scales

These scales contain only five notes. The name *pentatonic* is derived from the Greek word *penta*, which means five. They use the root, 2nd, major 3rd, 5th and 6th degrees of the major scale.

C pentatonic scale

Track 2-35 is the demonstration at the faster tempo (♩ = 104), **Track 2-36** is the slowed down backing track (♩ = 92), then **Track 2-37** is the backing track at full speed.

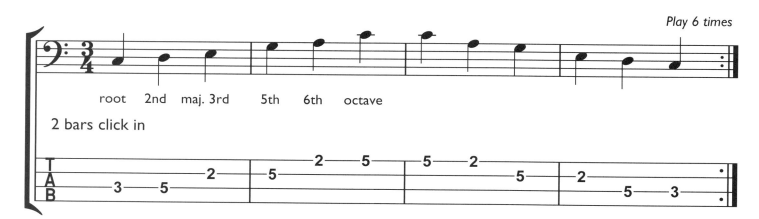

root   2nd   maj. 3rd   5th   6th   octave

2 bars click in

Play 6 times

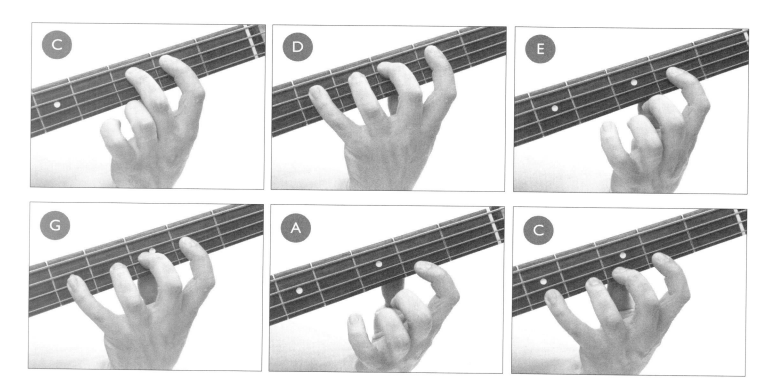

C D E G A C

Tip

Try this scale at the 8th fret of the E string and at the 15th fret of the A string, as we did with C major.

The blues using the pentatonic scale

In this 12 bar blues sequence we use a bass riff derived from the pentatonic scale. The line uses the root, major 3rd, 5th and 6th degrees of the pentatonic scale, missing only the 2nd (D).

C pentatonic riff

Listen to **Track 2-38** first, and then move on to **Track 2-39** to play along with the band.

Practice track 38 in the key of C, then transpose the riff to the key of F starting on fret 8 of the A string. For the key of G, start the riff at fret 10 of the A string.

▶ **Tommy Shannon – played bass with Stevie Ray Vaughan**

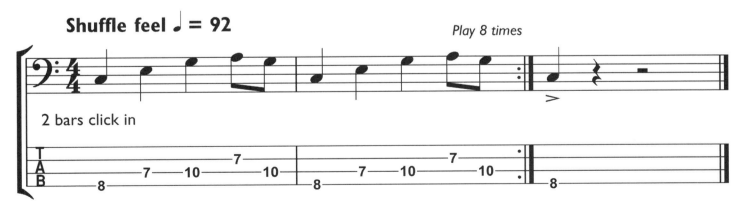

Shuffle feel ♩ = 92

Play 8 times

2 bars click in

The pentatonic scale

Donald "Duck" Dunn has played with The Blues Brothers, Eric Clapton and Booker T.

The four bar "tag"

In *Absolute Beginners Bass Guitar* (Book One), we covered the 12 bar blues sequence in the keys of A and E. This time we are in the key of C playing a shuffle feel pattern. We practiced the shuffle feel earlier in track 5.

Here, the blues sequence is a combination of the three riffs in C (track 38), F and G. In order to round things off, we have a four bar "tag" to finish as shown below. This repeats the last four bars of the sequence, adding a nifty little chromatic phrase to end. Listen to the tag in **Track 2-40** and then play along with **Track 2-41.**

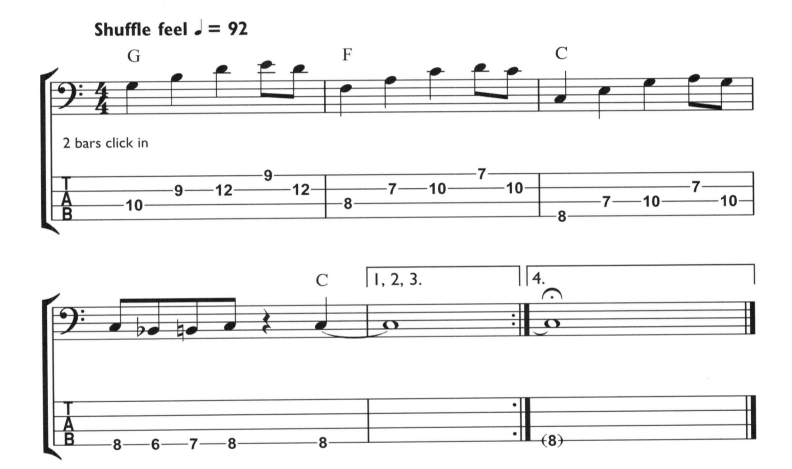

Putting it all together

Let's put what we've learned over the last few pages together to make a full 12 bar blues sequence with a four bar tag ending.

Listen to **Track 2-42** over the page, then move on to **Track 2-43** to play along with the band.

12 bar blues shuffle in C

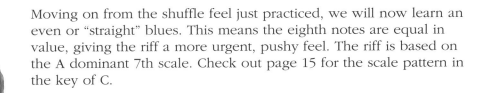

Moving on from the shuffle feel just practiced, we will now learn an even or "straight" blues. This means the eighth notes are equal in value, giving the riff a more urgent, pushy feel. The riff is based on the A dominant 7th scale. Check out page 15 for the scale pattern in the key of C.

We also need to practice the riff in the keys of D (4th degree of the scale, or chord IV) and E (5th degree of the scale, or chord V) to complete the 12 bar sequence. Here is the riff that we will be working with. It uses the root, octave, flatted 7th, and 5th degrees of the dominant 7th scale.

Listen to **Track 2-44** to get into the groove, and then turn to **Track 2-45** to play along.

2 bars click in

Tip

You need to be accurate with your plucking fingers or pick to execute this cleanly.

Straight eight blues in A

This blues in A is based on the riff we learned playing tracks 44 and 45. You will need to transpose it to two other keys, D and E, to complete the sequence. This time you can do it yourself; remember that D is chord IV and E is chord V. On the last bar of the sequence (bar 12) we "pedal" eighth notes on E to go with the drums.

This gives a strong V to I cadence – that's E (V) to A (I). At the end there is a four bar tag, as in the shuffle blues. In bar 4 of the tag we play an A major arpeggio to end (check out the C major arpeggio on page 13). Just transpose the C major pattern to A.

Cue up **Track** 2-46 for the demo and then play with the band on **Track** 2-47.

The slide

Before we tackle our next groove we need to look at a new device which can be added to our bass lines to help create a happening vibe. The slide (sometimes called *glissando* – or *gliss.* for short) can be used as a fill into a section or as a smooth transition between notes. It can be small, between two adjacent notes, or big, helping to accentuate a drum fill or phrase. It is notated as a straight line going up or down between the notes affected.

Placement

The first slide is on the upbeat. Hit the start note A (12th fret, A string) and slide down to D (5th fret, A string). Play the next slide on beat 4 of bar 2 going up from D to A again.

Listen to the demonstration on **Track 2-48**, and then try it yourself in **Track 2-49**.

Slide from A on 12th fret, A string...

...to D on 5th fret, A string.

Tip

Keep the string pressed down on the fingerboard to get a clean slide.

Adam Clayton, U2

You too

Track 2-50 shows the quarter note slide used in a song – think U2 for this style of playing. Make sure your eighth notes are played long with no gaps in between them and practice your slides so they reach their destination right on the beat. In the verse, all of the notes are on the A string.

In the bridge, use the D on fret 5 of the A string to get to the high D at fret 12 on the D string.

Coming down, stay on the D string until the 5th fret, then switch to the D on the A string again (5th fret). Have a slippery time with this one!

Once you've mastered this, play along with **Track 2-51**.

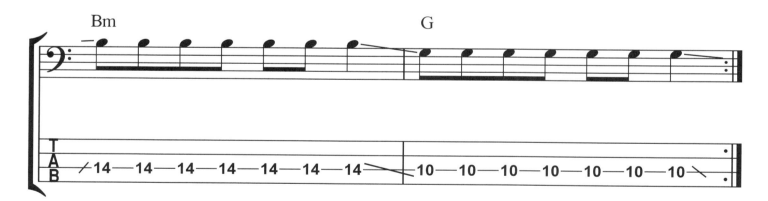

Bridge

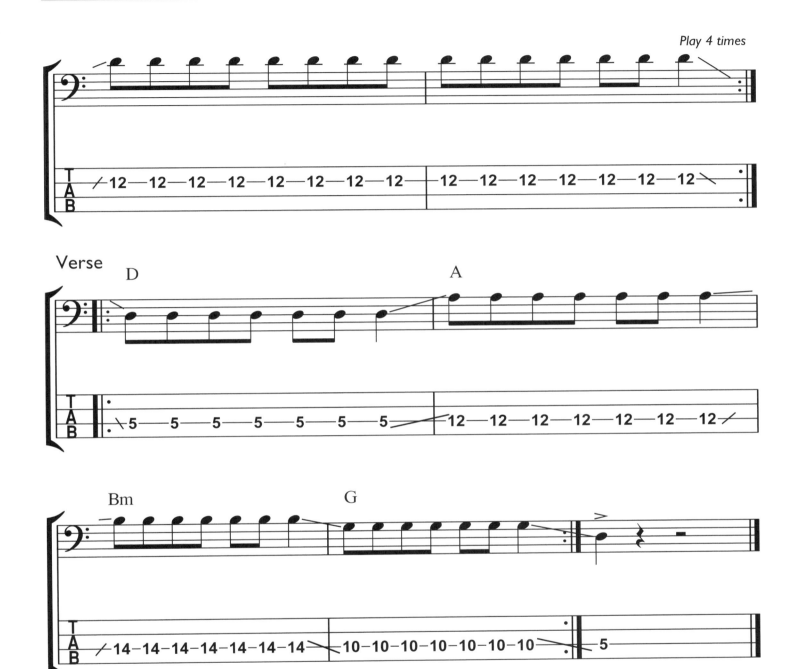

Heavy rock/blues scale

In this section we get lowdown and heavy. We are going to be using a riff based on the *blues* scale. This is a scale used frequently in rock and blues music and consists of the root, minor 3rd, 4th, flatted 5th, natural 5th and flatted 7th. The flatted 5th and flatted 7th give it a rocky, demonic flavor.

Even though it contains a minor 3rd, it can be used over a variety of chords, including "5" chords (root, 5th and octave rock guitar chords, also called "power chords").

Listen to **Track 2-52** to hear what it sounds like and then play along with **Track 2-53**

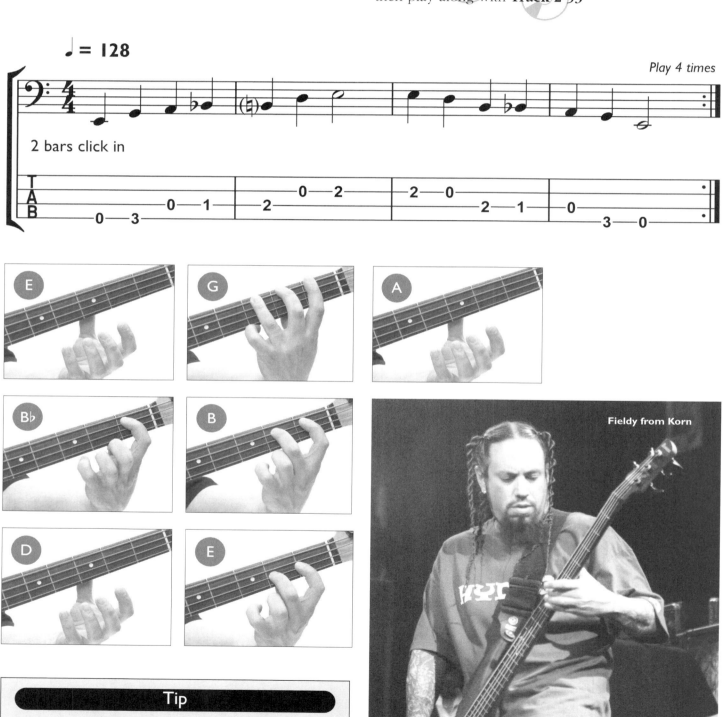

Fieldy from Korn

Tip

Hold the eighth notes for their full value to get that big rock sound!

Track 2-54 is the same scale again but played in the higher position.

Listen to and then play along with **Track 2-**

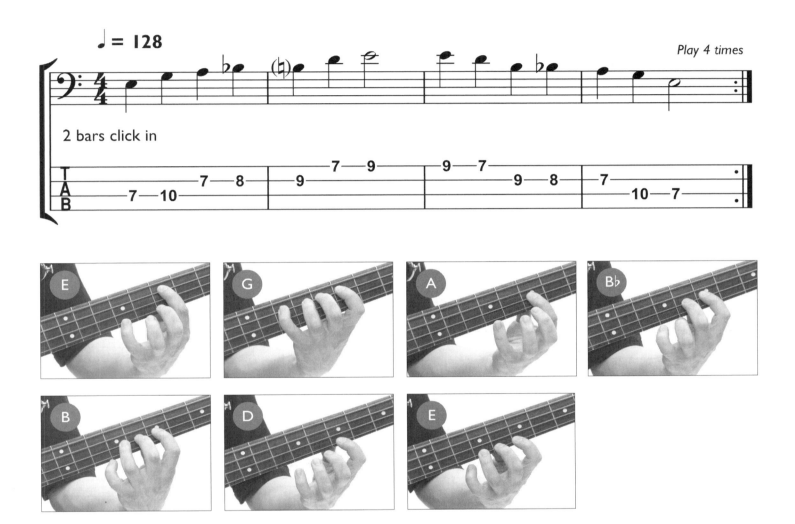

Track 2-56 over the page is an example of how to use the blues scale in a heavy rock setting.

Watch out – the riff is played at double the speed of tracks 52 and 54.

The bridge section is in the key of A and uses the root, minor 3rd, and 4th degrees of the blues scale.

55. Practice the whole blues scale in A before you start.

Once you feel confident, play along with **Track 2-57.**

Accents
In bars 4 and 8 of the bridges, there are some accents. This is notated by a > above the notes affected. Play these notes a little harder than normal. Dig in!

Rock out

Bridge solo

Last verse/Last 8

Play 4 times

Equipment

The bass player's tool kit

Now that we are getting more organized in our approach, we need to get our gear together so it always performs the way we want it to.

In rehearsal and gig situations there are some equipment essentials to make life easier when things go wrong.

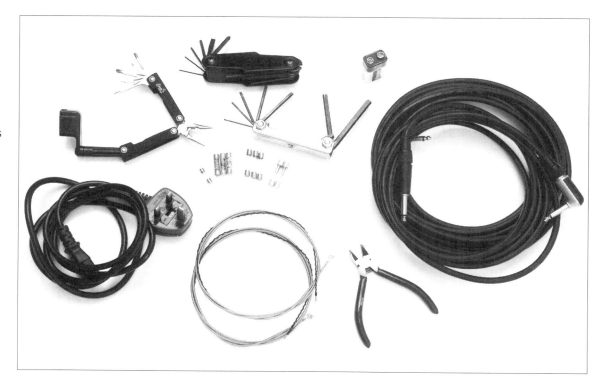

Strings
Always have a spare set on you, even if they are your old ones.

Wire cutters
Keep these in your bag with the strings. If there is too much winding on the tuning keys you can trim down the ends.

Allen keys
The truss rod, in the neck and the bridge saddles, normally has Allen head screws for adjustment. You can get a set of Allen keys for these from a good bike shop. For the small bridge saddle types try a hardware store. There are also guitar tool sets, which have most sizes in them.

Instrument cables
Buy the best cables you can afford. They last longer and sound better. Monster Cable, Planet Waves, Switchcraft and Neutrik all sell great products. Always carry a spare too.

Speaker cables
If you don't use a combo amp you will need speaker cables. As with the instrument cables, get the best you can. There are quite a few different types of speaker plugs. If yours are not standard, keep a spare in your bag, just in case. Never use an instrument cable or microphone cable.

Power cords
These are of standard quality and usually supplied with the amp. Do carry a spare though, as this is another potential gig stopper! Always carry an extension cord, just in case there are no plugs near you at the venue.

Batteries
You will need two types. One for your tuner and another for your bass if it has active electronics. Always carry a spare 9-volt (the usual size for a bass) especially if your bass has no passive back up. Once your bass runs out of juice so does your performance, so buy the best batteries you can!

Phillips/Posidrive screwdriver
Have one of these in your bag of the correct size for the screws in your bass. You won't get the battery out without one and you will wreck the screw heads using anything else.

Fuses
A small selection of plug and amp (glass type) fuses could save your gig. Check the rating on the back of your amp and open your plug to see if it contains 3, 5 or 13 amps.

Dust cloths
These are great for wiping down the strings after gigs. Make sure you wipe down the underside of the strings too.

Dominant 7th riff

Let's get down with a funky eighth note riff in the style of James Brown and The Average White Band. The riff is based around an F7 chord. It uses the root, flatted 7th and natural 6th of the F dominant 7th scale. Bar 2 of the riff repeats the first two and a half beats. It then adds two eighth notes on beat 3+ and beat 4. The Ab to A♮ gives a funky chromatic resolution to the riff.

Rests!

The riff is a two-bar pattern and has a rest at the end of bar 1. The rests are just as important as the notes! Lock into the drums and guitar and keep your notes short to help accentuate the groove. Counting "1 and 2 and 3 and 4 and" will help you feel the rests.

Listen carefully to **Track 2-58** then play along with **Track 2-59**.

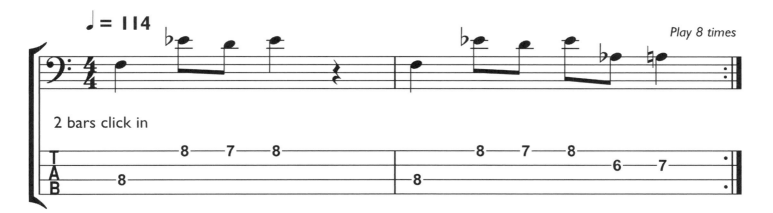

It's now time to put our two-bar funk riff into a song. We are using the riff from track 58 in four different keys: F, Bb, Ab and Db. The riff makes up the intro and verse patterns.

The bridge uses the riff in Ab and Db for a bar each. It then has a two-bar eighth note build on a C under a C7sus4 chord. Drop down to *mp* as indicated and build through the next two bars. On beat 4 of the last bar of the bridge, we have a quarter note C sliding up to the end. This C (V) to F (I) gives a strong V to I cadence.

Watch the very last bar in which we miss the downbeat and play on beat 2.

Turn over the page and check out **Track 2-60** then play along with the band in **Track 2-61**.

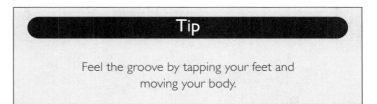

Tip

Feel the groove by tapping your feet and moving your body.

74 Funky groove

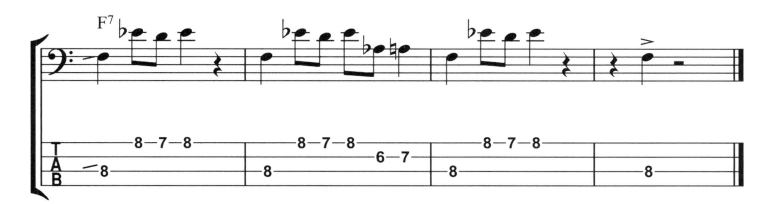

Syncopation

In order to make our bass lines funkier, we need to add another flavor into our funk melting pot. Track 60 had an "on" beat feel throughout. **Track 2-62** takes us into new territory – the bass line is phrased "off" the beat.

This is known as a *syncopated* line. You will need to count "1 and 2 and 3 and 4 and" to feel this line correctly. By playing off the beat, our notes land on the "and" (&) part of the beat each time. Listen carefully to the demo and then get uptight and funky with the band in **Track 2-63**.

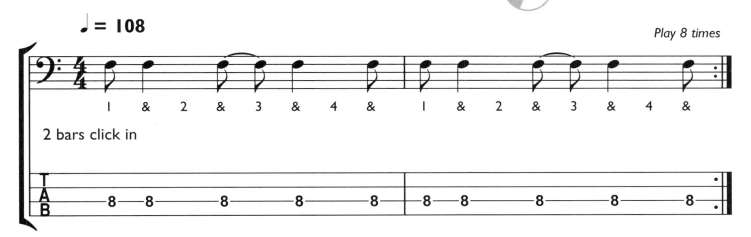

In the song over the page we bring together all that we have learned in the "funk" section.

The riff in the verse is now over four bars. It is three bars from the riff in track 60, then a bar of syncopation from track 62. The fourth bar of the riff is chromatic over an F7 chord using the root, major 3rd, 4th, flatted 5th and natural 5th.

The bridge is similar to track 60 except in bar 2 where we have the chromatic syncopated riff in Db. In bar 4 of the bridge we have a *staccato* (short) C quarter note on beat 1 and then three beats on an accented (>) half note, so hold it until the end of the bar.

At the end we play an F7 arpeggio in a syncopated rhythm but with shorter eighth notes. Play the root, major 3rd, 5th, flatted 7th and octave. The last note (F) is on the "and" of beat 1 in the very last bar.

Listen carefully to **Track 2-64** then play along with **Track 2-65**.

Get down and funky

Bridge

(Play verse 3 times)

Slap pattern – the thumb

The thumb

In this last section we are going to get our thumb out and get funky in the style of Red Hot Chili Peppers and Jamiroquai.

Accuracy

First we need to make sure we are using our thumb in the correct way.

Hit the E string with the outside edge of your thumb. See the pictures below for your top and front view. You need to hit the string down onto the metal frets near the end of the fingerboard.

Top view

Front view

Hit the string hard and move your thumb away quickly, allowing the string to vibrate freely. The thumb slap is notated with a "T" under the notehead.

Listen to **Track 2-66** to hear a funk slap pattern and then try it yourself with the band in **Track 2-67**.

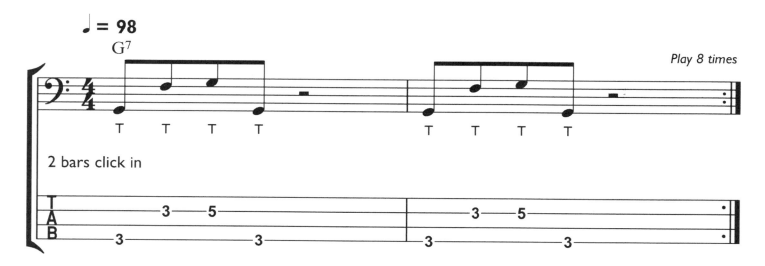

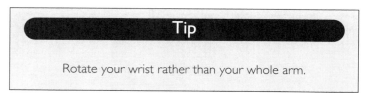

Tip

Rotate your wrist rather than your whole arm.

The pull

We've done the slap, now let's do the pull! The pull is notated with a "P" under the note affected.

Accuracy

You need to curl your finger under the string to get a good pull. Don't be afraid to pull the string hard away from the fingerboard. It needs to snap back against the frets to get the best sound. In the example below, the pull is on the G string. It is easier to pull this string as there is no string below it.

The pattern below consists of the note C being played up and down in octaves. This will remind you of disco bass lines from the seventies, so check out some Larry Graham or Rose Royce tracks, particularly the chorus in "Car Wash." So slap the C on the A string (3rd fret) and then pull the octave C on the G string (fifth fret).

The diagrams below show you how the pull should look. You can either use your index or middle finger.

Top view

Front view

Check out **Track 2-68** to hear how it's played then try for yourself with the band in **Track 2-69**.

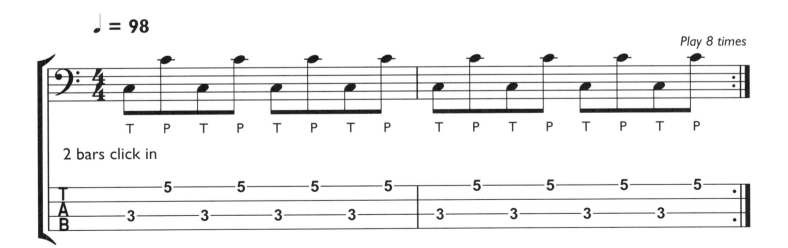

Moving octaves

In the next example, we use the same rhythm as in track 68 except we are moving between C octaves and B♭ octaves.

Keep your hand in the same octave shape and move up and down from C (3rd fret, A string) to B♭ (1st fret, A string) and octave B♭. Check the diagrams below for your hand position on the fingerboard.

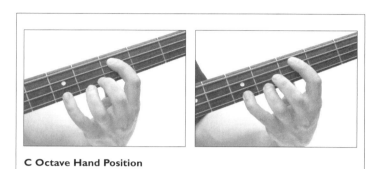

C Octave Hand Position

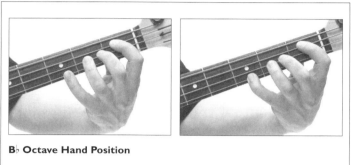

B♭ Octave Hand Position

When you've got this down, check out **Track 2-70** then groove along with the band in **Track 2-71**.

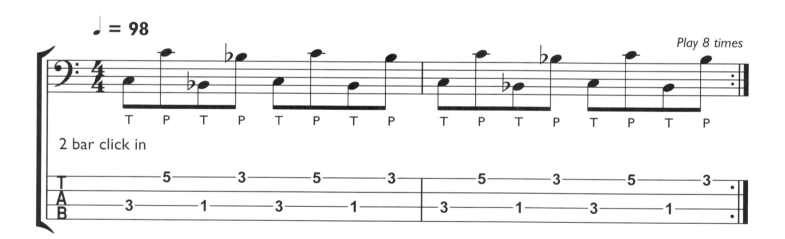

$\bullet = 98$

Play 8 times

T P T P T P T P   T P T P T P T P

2 bar click in

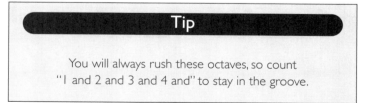

Tip

You will always rush these octaves, so count "1 and 2 and 3 and 4 and" to stay in the groove.

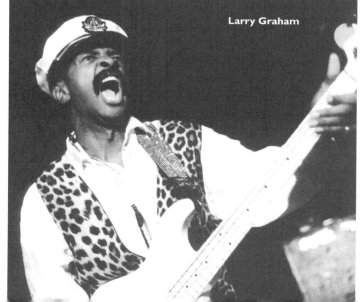

Larry Graham

This next song over the page brings together the slap and pull funk section in a snappy two-bar riff. Bar 1 is from track 66 with the addition of two B♭ eighth notes on beat 3 and a quarter note C on beat 4. These are all played with the thumb.

Bar 2 is again the first two beats from track 66, this time adding two beats of octaves from track 70 on C and B♭.

Check out **Track 2-72** for the whole thing, and then try it yourself in **Track 2-73**.

Gail Ann Dorsey has played with the likes of David Bowie and Tears For Fears.

Slappin' funk

In this last example we are going to bring together all that we have covered in the book, which kind of gives us a funk, rock, slap, pentatonic, blues scale sort of song! Good luck!

Intro
Similar to track 62 in its rhythm, and bar 5 of track 64 in notation.

Verse 1
Like the two-bar riff we heard in track 60. Watch out for the quarter note slide from bar 4 into bar 5.

Bridge 1/Rock
Four-bar pattern based on the verse of track 56 with eighth notes on E to break up the riff.

Slap Chorus 1
This two-bar pattern uses the riffs from tracks 66 and 70 plus a chromatic octave climb. Bar 8 of the chorus has two accented (>) quarter notes on beats 3 and 4. Hit them hard and make them short.

Verse 2
As verse 1, then modulates to D9 for a bar, then to G7sus4. The two-bar riff changes from D to G. Watch the quick position change.

Bridge 2/Rock
Identical to bridge 1.

Middle Eight
Use your blues scale in E and pentatonic scale in C here. Bar 8 is similar to bar 1 of the intro.

Verse 3
Identical to verse 1.

Slap Chorus 2
The first six bars are identical to slap chorus 1. Bars 7 and 8 contain an offbeat C7 arpeggio building in intensity.

Now turn over the page and listen to **Track 2-74** carefully; practice, and then play along with the band in **Track 2-75**.

Ninth chords
You may spot that after many of the chords, the number "9" appears. This tells us the chord has a 9th added to it. In the case of C, this adds a D above the 8th note of the scale.

The 9th chord consists of the root, major 3rd, 5th, flatted 7th and natural 9th. If you can, play this on a keyboard to hear the voicing.

Here's what it looks like:

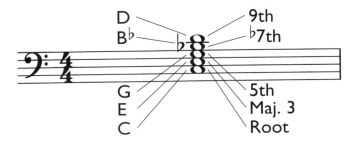

Mix it up!

$\quad$ = 112

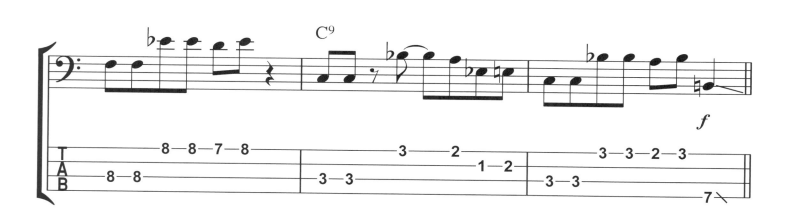

Bridge 1/Rock

Bridge 2/Rock

Middle 8

Verse 3

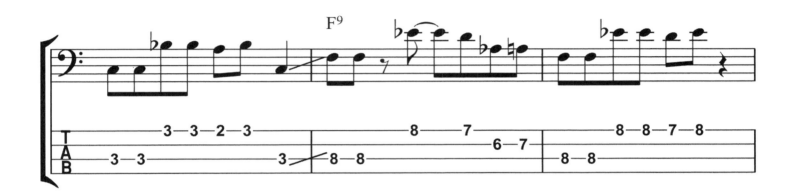

Slap Chorus 2

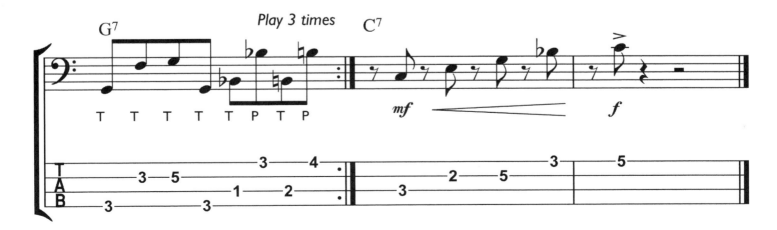

Congratulations!

You've made good progress and have built on the basic skills needed to express yourself on the bass.

To make the most of your new techniques be sure to practice regularly and check out as much new music as possible.

To remove your CD from the plastic sleeve, lift the small lip to break the perforations.

Replace the disc after use for convenient storage.

FINAL CHECKPOINT
WHAT YOU HAVE ACHIEVED.

You can now:
- Tune up from a single note
- Practice in an organized fashion
- Play scales and arpeggios in different positions
- Use and understand the pentatonic and blues scales
- Play eighth note bass lines using the slide
- Play eighth note funk bass lines with syncopation
- Play eighth note rock bass lines
- Use the slap and pull in your bass lines

ABSOLUTE BEGINNERS
Guide To Bass

The Fingerboard

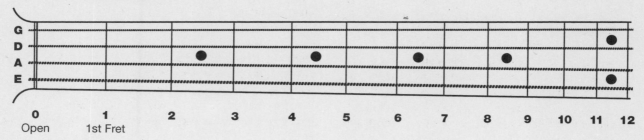

The Notes

Tablature

Tablature, or tab notation, runs in parallel with the standard staff, and gives additional information specific to the bass guitar. Think of it as a drawing of the neck of your bass, where the four horizontal lines represent the strings, the lowest line being for the E string, the highest being for the G string. The numbers written on these lines represent the fret positions on the fingerboard.

Notice that tab gives us only string and fret information. It doesn't tell us anything about rhythm, dynamics (loudness) or pitch as such.

Staff notation gives us a full musical picture, whereas tab is only an aid to playing the bass. Of course when you run the two in tandem you do get the complete picture.

Tuning

The first thing to do when you strap on your bass is to tune it. Nowadays it is normal to have an electronic tuning device of some kind, but it is still important for you to understand and to be able to tune it without an external reference. You will find this particularly useful when the battery in your electronic tuner dies!

Tuning By Harmonics

Harmonics, simply put, are a series of overtones which are present in any vibrating string. When fretting a harmonic, both portions of the string, behind and in front of the finger, must be free to vibrate. Therefore the finger is not actually pressed into the fingerboard, but simply rests lightly on the string.

Try this on frets 5 and 7 until you get a clear bell-like tone. The harmonic on the 5th fret of the E (lowest) string is the same harmonic as the 7th fret of the A string. If you play them together you will have some idea of whether the strings are in tune with each other.

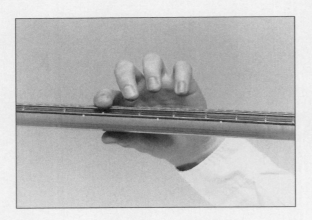

First of all you must check that the open E string (the string you start tuning from) is in tune with the other instruments, or the CD you are playing along with. Once you are satisfied that the E is in tune, you can play the harmonic at the 5th fret to check the next string. Let this harmonic ring and play the harmonic on the 7th fret of the A string.

The two harmonics will now be heard together. If they combine to make one pure tone you're in luck—they are in tune!

If there is an oscillation (a regular beating sound) going on between them the A string will have to be adjusted until there is a pure tone. If the oscillations are fast the notes are fairly wide apart.

The closer the tuning gets the slower the beating becomes. You have to judge whether the harmonic on the A string is higher or lower than the harmonic on the E string.

Once the A string is tuned to the E string you have to repeat the process twice, tuning the D string to the A string, and then the G string to the D string. When each harmonic at the 5th fret in tune with its adjacent higher string at the 7th fret, your bass is in tune.

Tuning By Full Notes

Harmonics are not the only way to tune your bass—you can use full notes as well. Tune your E string to a reference instrument or CD. Once again the low E becomes the reference point from which all other tuning is done.

Having tuned the low E we can tune the A string by playing an A on the 5th fret of the E string and comparing its tuning with that of the open E string. As before we will hear either a pure tone if the strings are in tune, or an oscillation if they are not.

As the notes draw closer together the oscillations (or ringing) will slow down gradually until they disappear completely, at which point the strings are in tune. The process is repeated for the rest of the strings.

Hand Positions

The Fretting Hand

First of all, relax your fretting hand—this is most important as a relaxed hand will prevent tension-related pain in the wrist and fingers.

Shake your hand and arm, allowing your arm to fall down by your side. Your hand will automatically assume a relaxed and natural position.

As a general rule it is good to use one finger for each fret, as pictured. Your fingers should be spaced out and relaxed, with the thumb behind the middle and index fingers.

Although this may help in the short term, bunching up your fingers in this way will prevent the development of individual finger strength, reach and flexibility.

There is no easy way to acquire a good technique. It is good practice to keep your 'spare' fretting fingers (i.e. those which are not actually fretting a note) in contact with the fingerboard at all times. This is a classical cello player's technique.

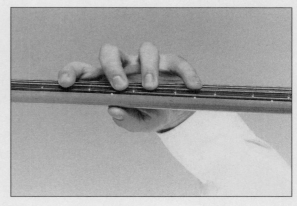

Move your hand to a playing position, as pictured. At first you may find it difficult to relax while applying pressure to the strings. This will improve as your hand and fingers gain strength. Don't bunch your fingers together in an attempt to exert the necessary pressure on the strings.

Holding The Bass

The height at which you hold the bass is a matter of personal choice, though it is true to say that for rock music the bass is slung low, while for funk and slap styles it is worn significantly higher.

There are no set rules to dictate where you should hold your bass, but be practical. Try to keep a relaxed posture with a straight back. Keep your shoulders back, otherwise you will suffer from fatigue and thereby shorten the time span during which you are able to play in comfort.

If you play standing up but practice sitting down, it is a good idea to still wear your strap when sitting. This will keep your bass in the same position, relative to your body, as when you are standing.

Methods Of Plucking:

Fingers

There is no set method for finger plucking, though it is obviously better to have some logic in your action rather than a random approach. You can use any or all of your fingers, though most people find it effective to use the first and second fingers, alternately. The third finger doesn't have the same independence of movement as the first two, and is better avoided until later.

The picture shows a typical example of the placement of your plucking hand. Try to anchor on something solid like the side of a pickup or the scratchplate. Practice playing the A (second lowest) string alternately with your first and second fingers.

The Pick

The pick is a shaped piece of material, usually plastic or metal, which is used to pluck the strings of the bass. It comes in various thicknesses, or gauges, so you should be able to find one to suit your personal taste.

Because the pick is made of a material harder than the flesh of your fingers, the sound it produces from the bass is more sharply defined. This is especially popular in rock styles where a hard-edged 'clicky' sound is needed to kick the music along.